Dedicated to all the young girls who stand out in a normal world. These are the words I needed to hear when I was your age. You have a superpower that is meant to be shared with the world.

Don't allow this world to dim your light.

♡ Nat

Dear Young Differently-Abled Girl

by Nathalie Calderon

The day you were born

you changed the world.

Every person you meet

is forever transformed.

A rare light within you,

you don't often see.

A strength beyond words,

and a sparkle that's unique.

Your journey may not look
like other kids,
And they may do things
that you wish you did.
Sometimes you'll think
that life is unfair,
And wish for change
through continuous prayers.

Keep your head up
'cause this world can seem mean,
People fear what
they don't normally see.
Don't take it personally,
they mean you no harm.
They're learning from you
how to open their hearts.

I'm here to tell you
not to lose hope,
Because your differences are
what makes you dope.

It's okay to cry sometimes
to let the hurt out.
Those tears help the seeds
of happiness sprout.

Don't take what they say
"you can" or "can't do."
They tell you THEIR fears,
what THEY think YOU can't do.

If it's something you want,

just put you mind to it.

This is <u>YOUR</u> life,

only <u>YOU</u> can live through it!

From the days when you're feeling

sad, down and low...

...to the days when you're Queen
at the self-love disco.

Look in the mirror

and tell yourself this

Everyday to attract

peace, love and happiness:

I'm an intelligent
and a beautiful girl.
I can achieve
anything in the world.
All strengths that I need
are possessed within me.
I love who I am
and what makes me unique.

I'm enough, I'm worthy
of all that I want.
I'm a loved, cherished diamond,
I'm the jackpot!

I'm a masterpiece

that only gets better with time.

My existence is royal

and spiritually divine.

I'm bright as a sun

giving light to the night,

I'm as free as a bird

in the sky taking flight.

My different ability

won't define me.

I'm one-of-a-kind,

being authentically me!

If ever you feel like

these words don't ring true,

Remember all these things

are ultimately you.

Your past, your present

and your future self

Has the power to accomplish

nothing less.